How to Analyze People

How to Read Anyone Like a Book

By Madison Taylor

Table of Contents

Introduction

Wouldn't it be nice to be able to read people like books? You could know their hidden intentions and true feelings. You could avoid all miscommunication and deception. The guesswork would be taken out of social interaction. This sounds like a dream come true, right?

While it is not possible to read minds, you can get pretty close to clairvoyance with the tips in this book. This book is your guide to the fundamentals of reading people like books. You will learn everything you need to know about body language, facial expressions, nuances of speech, and other signs that reveal what a person is trying to conceal.

It may seem very difficult to figure out what a person is trying to hide. People may seem like obscure, impenetrable mysteries. But that is just because you don't know the cues and signs to watch for. Once you learn them, reading people is actually very easy.

Some people make a living out of reading others. FBI profilers, cops, job interviewers, and even dating profile matchmakers are excellent reads of character who are adroit at finding out who people really are without being told. These people are not in possession of some secret superhuman talent. Rather, they have mastered tips and tricks that you can master yourself. This book will help you become as good as an FBI profiler at reading other people.

You first have to learn some of the main tells that people exhibit. These tells not only betray when someone is lying, but they also indicate what a person is not saying. Tells give away what a person is hiding inside, whether or not the person is being dishonest. One of the best tells is any inconsistency between someone's talk and body language. Eye contact is another great tell. Fidgeting can indicate nervousness.

You can glean a lot of information about people by what they do directly say, however. People are surprisingly open. You just have to pay attention. Learning to read people involves learning to really listen and absorb what someone says to you.

Furthermore, you must learn to make people want to open up to you. You can make yourself the type of person that people want to talk to. You want to project an aura of caring and compassion that make others trust you and feel comfortable around you.

There are so many different ways to read people. From being introspective to carefully observing others, this book will cover them all.

You may wonder why reading people is so important. There are countless benefits to being able to understand the people around you right off the bat. Your understanding of people can certainly make your life easier.

For one thing, you can become a more sensitive and empathetic lover and friend because you understand people better. You can read the signs of someone's emotions and respond appropriately. You will no longer be clueless about what those around you feel.

You also can avoid a lot of pain and problems by learning to identify the true intentions of people. Some people are just bad. Most bad people are good at hiding it, however. You can see through their ruses and protect yourself. On the flip side, you can spot good people who will treat you well. As a result, you can avoid bad friends and pick good ones. Your dating life will improve as well as you become more discerning about your partners.

Work can become easier. If you work in sales or customer service, you will be able to read your customers for clues about whether or not they are happy. If you work for clients, you can understand their wants better. You can become more empathetic and understanding of co-workers and superiors. This can help you satisfy people that you work with better.

In addition, you will get along better with your family. By being able to read your family members, you can tell what they are feeling and what they expect. Fights over "nothing" will stop because you will be able to spot the warning signs that a fight is coming. You will also be more empathetic, which your family members will appreciate.

Even on the street, you can become more discerning about the intentions of others. You can spot people who mean you harm and take steps to protect yourself. This is quite important for self-defense.

The life skill of people reading is very helpful and essential to your success in your social life. Therefore, you should start learning today. You have started in the right place with this book.

Chapter 1: The Secrets to Reading People

Free Your Judgment

There are many things that can cloud your judgment when reading people. Biases, intimidation, and sexual attraction are just some of the things that can make you choose to ignore your gut and misread someone. You may think that someone's harsh actions are admirable if you admire the person, while their actions would appear despicable if you did not admire them. Do not let anything cloud your judgment.

Men are more likely to judge pretty young women less harshly. They let pretty young women get away with disrespectful behavior in hopes of winning their favor. If you are attracted to someone, you are more likely to ignore red flags about the person. Try to look past sexual attraction. Understand that there are plenty of attractive people in the world, so fixating on one person's attractiveness is not necessary. You just need to view an attractive person more objectively. Try to focus on his or her character as a separate thing from his or her looks.

Status or certain jobs can also make you admire someone. But understand that someone is not perfect just because of his or her status. Do not let someone's status intimidate you or bamboozle you. In fact, they probably got to where they are today by being cruel to others. Read their character separately from their status or work.

Being in your own emotional funk can really distort your judgment, too. When you are emotionally down, you may be harsher to judge others in your state of bitterness. You may also be more vulnerable to kind actions from others. Unfortunately, manipulators are great at spotting when you are upset and offering a kind action in order to gain favor with you. Do not let your emotional state make you vulnerable in judgment.

Emotional wounds can make it hard for you to trust people. This is especially true after you been through a divorce or bad break-up. As a result, you might judge the gender that you are attracted to unfairly. You may instantly dislike all people of that gender. Do not be so quick to write off people that you do not know. Use your scars as lessons to read people who remind you of those that have hurt you in the past, but do not make the mistake of thinking that the entire gender is bad. Give individuals a chance. Try to read them for who they are, not who your ex was.

Don't Just Base it Off of Behavior

Many people make the mistake of trying to read people off of behavior alone. But often behavior offers an incomplete and inaccurate picture. There is so much going on under the surface that you cannot reasonably read someone's inner turmoil based on their behavior alone. You must consider someone's biases, mood, and even the context of the situation. Often, you cannot know all of this information, so don't even attempt to read someone based off of behavior alone.

Sometimes behavior is inaccurate because it is fake. Many people are great at creating a façade. They appear totally normal and upstanding, while hiding their horrendous internal flaws. Think of most serial killers. Often they go to work, keep nice houses, and look like totally normal people. The world is shocked when they are finally caught with a basement full of hacked up bodies and torture devices. Sexual deviants who get caught watching child porn are often politicians and businessmen with great jobs and totally normal outside appearances. While these examples are extreme, many people are adept at hiding their bad personalities under totally normal behavior. Therefore, you cannot base judgments off of the outward behavior of others, as this behavior can be faked and misleading.

Create a Baseline

Try to gauge a baseline of someone's normal behavior. Watch for unusual mannerisms that a person often displays. Quirks and habits that you frequently observe in someone over time form the person's baseline. A baseline does not take long to form once you become more adept at reading people with practice. FBI profilers will usually gather this information within the first fifteen seconds of meeting a person.

From this baseline, you are able to tell when someone is behaving abnormally. When someone is behaving abnormally, you can determine that something is going on. Perhaps the person is lying or is upset about something.

It is difficult to start a baseline on someone if you do not have a chance to observe him over a period of time and you are not yet adept at reading people in just a few seconds. Therefore, it is a good idea to watch for really odd behavior. Behavior that stands out as unusual may be a quirk or it may be a sign of something more ominous, such as deception. You may want to ask other people who know the person well if this behavior is normal for him. If you can't do that, then you simply must rely on your gut. But do not rely too much on behavior to form judgments about people.

You can start a baseline just by asking someone how they are doing today. Watch how the person reacts. From there, you can determine what his or her normal mannerisms are. The more you talk, the more you can gather about the person's baseline. Does his eye tic often? Does he often gesticulate with his hands? Does he stutter normally, or is he normally articulate? Also gauge the speed with which he speaks in normal conversation and the tone and pitch of his voice.

You must establish a baseline in order to tell when someone is behaving inconsistently. In addition, a baseline lets you know how a person is in normal settings. If a person is typically nervous, you can decide if you want to be around someone who is frequently nervous and therefore probably insecure with social anxiety. If a person is typically rude and blunt, you can determine if you want to deal with that kind of behavior in the future.

Infer Things from the Initial Reaction

Of course, strangers tend to be tense in their initial behavior toward you because they do not know you well. But a person's initial reaction to you indicates a lot of information about how he feels about himself and how he feels about other people. This initial reaction shows the hang-ups he may have and the guard that he puts up to protect himself or the façade that he erects to charm people that he meets for the first time. As a result, this reaction says a lot about who he is as a person and the things that you may expect from him as you get to know him better.

If he is initially rude, for instance, he may thaw and become nicer toward you, but you know that at heart he has his guard up against new people. You can then wonder why he has his guard up. He is probably a sensitive and insecure person with a lot of emotional baggage; he feels that he has to act tough and careless in order to avoid getting hurt.

Particularly articulate and charming people usually have a lot to hide. They are great at being around people and hiding who they really are. They have designed behavior that is intended to hook people. Very charming behavior is often indicative of manipulative and deceptive personalities.

A person who is overly nervous usually has social anxiety and is rife with insecurities.

This person will probably get more comfortable with you over time. However, you may want to avoid trusting him too much. As a general rule, people who are insecure are not reliable and will act in ways that are not always appropriate. Insecure people tend to have trust issues and they will act out in ways that are hurtful because they believe that they are not good enough. You are not responsible for the insecurities of another person, so don't allow such a person to burden you with his problems and doubts.

A person who acts too calm is probably also a sufferer of social anxiety. However, he is adept at projecting calmness to hide how nervous he is. Become suspicious of people who are just "too chill."

Also watch for people who only want to talk about themselves. People who are obsessed with themselves and don't even try to ask you questions about yourself are typically very selfish. This behavior will not change with time.

Another behavior that will not change with time is someone who is negative, even on your first meeting. People like this are very toxic and will simply try to drag you down.

A person who talks about others shamelessly when he first meets you is also probably a chronic gossip. It is not normal for someone to start gossiping when he first meets you.

Positivity and enthusiasm are great signs in a person that you have just met. However, if someone talks too much of a big game and brags overly much, you can assume that this person is trying to impress you or even make up for something that he feels that he is lacking. Mild positivity and enthusiasm is a great sign, but being overly enthusiastic is not.

Confidence and assurance of one's self is a good sign in a stranger. A person who is willing to introduce himself to you, look you in the eye, and talk to you is usually secure in himself. He has developed good social skills and hence might be a more sensitive friend, lover, or work associate. While you want to be wary of people who are too smooth and charming, someone who acts normal yet confident is usually a good person to know.

Ask Pointed Questions

If you want to get to know someone, feel free to ask him questions about himself. He will probably volunteer a lot of the information that you want to know. You don't even have to ask him things to find out a lot of information about who he is as a person, what he likes, and what he is looking for from his association with you. This is why you should be a good listener, which I cover in the next chapter.

But if he does not volunteer what you want to know, then ask. It is best to ask pointed questions and to not be vague. If you are vague, you run the risk of miscommunication. As an adult, there is no use or time for games anymore. You know that you cannot be a mind reader and neither can anyone else. So ask what you want to know without shame.

You do not want appear like you are interrogating someone. Asking rapid-fire questions can really put a person off. Asking overly personal questions about someone's life, family, or personality is also off-putting. But do not be afraid to ask general, socially acceptable questions whenever there is a break in the conversation.

Monitor a person in how he answers your questions. Since you have already more or less established a good baseline, you can tell when there are inconsistencies in his responses. If his gestures, tone, pitch, or eye contact suddenly shifts away from his baseline, then you can tell that he is not being truthful or that a question makes him uncomfortable for some reason. You can change the subject or pursue it more, depending on your goal in communication with him.

Word Choice is Important

How a person talks indicates a lot about what he is feeling and thinking. Listen for key words that indicate his intentions and his basic state of mind. The words that he chooses say a lot about how he is as a human being and what he is really feeling at the moment. If you are meeting someone for the first time, remember that the initial meeting speaks volumes about who a person is inside. How he chooses to speak to you right off the bat indicates a lot about who he is generally.

Someone who uses very harsh, aggressive language is an aggressive person or else he is currently in an angry mood. You never want someone to show you anger when you first meet; this indicates that the person may have an anger management problem.

Someone who uses very vague wording is possibly passive aggressive and trying to skirt around a hard subject. This type of person is not able to be direct. Expect games and behavior like shirking responsibility. If this person wrongs you, he will probably never admit to it and apologize. If he has a problem with you, he will probably never tell you to your face, but rather will hint about it or tell everyone else how he feels except for you.

Another troubling sign is when someone repeatedly says sorry or seems to take the blame for things. This type of person is very sinecure and blames himself for everything.

Someone who uses conceited language, such as bragging about how he just won "another" award, indicates how proud he is of himself. Watch for people who brag too much about themselves. These people are usually narcissistic and egotistical or else they are over compensating for feelings of inadequacy.

A person who uses very critical language is probably an overly judgmental person or a perfectionist. Watch for someone who nitpicks everything. This is a trait that will not lessen with time. If anything, it will only grow worse with time.

Most people use "I" terms more frequently than any other. This is not a troubling sign, but someone who uses more "we" terms is a better team player who is looking to collaborate with you. Someone who uses more "you" terms is focused on you. This can be a great sign that someone is focused on pleasing you and getting to know you, or else it can be a worrisome sign that someone is trying to manipulate you. Watch for other word choices in order to tell the difference. If someone is asking you about what you like or who you are, then that is usually a sign that he wants to get to know you or find out how to best please you. This is a great sign in a date, a new friend, or a person that you are thinking about hiring for a service. But if he seems to be fishing for pertinent information with overly personal questions, if he keeps trying to find ways that he can commiserate with you so that you will confide in him, or if he is using fancy language and flattery to make you feel ingratiated and charmed by him, then that is a bad sign that he is trying to get an emotional hook into you in order to manipulate you.

A good sign that someone is being shifty is vague language. Someone who refuses to answer yes or no questions is probably lying. Someone who uses confusing language is probably deliberately creating a sort of mirage of vagueness in order to hide something.

What is Unsaid Says a Lot

Studies suggest that ninety-three percent of human communication is unspoken. Since this is such a huge topic, I have dedicated an entire chapter to reading the tonality, body language, eye contact, and other nonverbal cues of other people for clues about what they are really trying to say. You can gather a lot of information about people from what they don't directly say, so read on to Chapter 4.

Chapter 2: Becoming a Better Listener

Becoming a better listener is the best thing that you can do when you want to read people. People are not always great at communication. Without meaning to, they often miscommunicate their needs or wants. But if you are very careful and astute listener, you can find out all the clues that people leave around and create a more complete picture of what people are trying to say to you. By becoming a better listener, you also make people want to open up to you. They will want to talk to you more and tell you things. You will become the person that everyone wants to confide in, and then you will bear a lot of pertinent information about people.

Create an Aura of Caring

If you project that you care, people will trust you and feel at ease around you. They will be more inclined to talk to you and confess intimate things to you. Creating this image that you are a caring person involves making yourself look trustworthy and interested.

Body language is important in this endeavor. You should also lean toward the person who is talking. Hold eye contact. Nod now and then. You can cross your legs to indicate that you feel comfortable, but avoid crossing your arms as this makes you appear closed off. Try having a more open stance instead, with your chest facing the person that is speaking to you. Of course always look at the speaker with a normal level of eye contact to show your deference in listening.

You also want to show genuine interest. Nodding is one way to do this. Frequently murmur in an assenting or sympathetic way. You can input enough of your own words to keep the conversation going, but it is important to not talk too much. The focus needs to be on the other person.

Stop talking about yourself. As a human being, you will want to talk about yourself. It is natural. But to be a good listener, you should keep the entire conversation focused on the other person, at least while he or she is talking. Not talking about yourself or constantly trying to turn the conversation onto yourself will make you appear like a better listener.

Mirroring is another way that you can make someone feel at ease around you. I will cover mirroring more in the next section.

Mirroring

You can set people at ease by mirroring their physical movements. Basically you just want to copy whatever someone does during conversation. If someone leans forward, lean forward about four seconds later. If someone leans back in his seat, lean back in your seat.

Matching your breath to the same rhythm as someone else's is a subliminal form of mirroring that often will set a person at ease. The person won't even know why he feels so comfortable around you. But he will and he will open up.

It may be hard to do this if you are not close to someone. Just notice when his chest fills with air and inhale at the same time. When his nostrils inflate with exhalation, exhale as well.

Ask Questions

Get a person to talk about himself. Since people love to talk about themselves, asking lots of questions will make people happy in conversation. Keep the conversation focused on the other person and ask him plenty of questions to keep him going. If he is telling you about work, for instance, be sure to ask lots of questions about his job. Keep your questions calm and insert them at natural moments or lulls in the conversation to avoid looking like you are interrogating him.

If someone is passionate about something, definitely start asking him questions about his passion. This is a great way to get someone to open up to you. It also makes people want to talk to you. You can get to know people just by finding out what they like and then asking a few questions about it to get them talking.

Asking also is better than mind reading. If you want to understand someone, ask him what he is thinking. Ask him what he really means when he says something that you don't quite understand. Don't attempt to play the mind reading game because this is how miscommunication can arise. Clear all miscommunication by asking questions instead.

Reduce Distractions

Nothing makes you look like you don't care as much as you being distracted. Put your phone away. Don't stare at the TV. Don't stare out the window or try to eavesdrop on other people. Give your full attention to the person that you are currently speaking to. Everyone that you speak to will feel valued and appreciated as a result. You will become more liked.

You will also free yourself of distractions so that you can devote all of your energy to the conversation. This makes you a better conversationalist. You are better able to listen and retain information. You are better able to remember what is said. You can think of appropriate responses to keep the conversation from going flat or awkward.

Summarize What was Said

After a person tells you something, it can help to offer a recap to show that you were listening and to make sure that you got everything understood correctly. Your summary can be brief; you don't have to regurgitate the entire conversation. But a brief recap can help both you and the other party assure that you listened well and the conversation was properly understood. It also assures the other party that you cared enough to reiterate.

Recognize what is Unsaid

A large part of human communication is silent. What someone does not say in person is often said in other subtle ways, such as through sighs, long pauses, tear-glistening eyes, raised or lowered tone and pitch of voice, and tense body language. Notice when someone is not saying and ask if everything is OK. If the person doesn't want to talk about what he is not saying, then don't press the issue. But carefully watch his body language and eye contact to try to gauge what he is not telling you. I will cover using body language to read people more in Chapter 4.

Don't Think Ahead

You may race to think ahead about what to say next. You think that you know how the conversation will go and what the person will say next, so you think that you can decide what to say ahead of time. Unfortunately, you are not a mind reader. Your predictions will often prove inaccurate. Prevent confusion or embarrassment by holding your tongue. Only decide what to say when it is your turn to speak. Then you know what was fully said and you are able to make an informed and suitable response.

Be Careful about Interrupting

Typically, it is wise to never interrupt. When you interrupt someone, you invalidate what he is saying. You can insult and even anger people by interrupting them. It is best to just wait your turn to speak.

However, there are times when you must speak out of turn. One good time is when the person you are speaking to begins to get overly emotional. You should interrupt politely to offer him reassurance and tell him that he should not be so upset. Another time is when someone is talking about making a very foolish mistake. You can interrupt to offer cautionary advice. But be sure to only pick times when it is necessary to interrupt. Otherwise, avoid doing so, no matter how excited you are to jump in with what you have to say.

Determine if You Should Add Input

Sometimes, it is OK to just sit there and listen. Few people ever do this, so you will stand out as a good listener should you do this. By being silent, you allow the person you are speaking to the opportunity to unabashedly open up. He can vent and tell you all and you will absorb it all.

Other times, your input is required. People rely on for advice, for instance, or they need you to offer some words to show your interest. Wait for certain pauses in conversation when the person seems expectant. This is when you should add input.

A friendly conversation or a conversation where you are trying to get to know someone is usually a back and forth. This is when your input is absolutely required. You seem like a stick in the mud if you don't contribute to such conversations. A conversation where someone is explaining something to you or venting about his life is when your silence is required.

As a human being, you have certain social instincts. You should follow these instincts. You also know the person that you are speaking to and the nature of your conversation the best. Listen to your gut about when to speak and what to say.

Remember Things

Remembering what people say to you is a crucial part of listening. If you can reiterate what someone says to you later on, you can prove that you were listening. You can continue the conversation where it was left off if you get cut off. You can also retain important information that someone imparts to you about him- or herself.

It is easier to remember everything when you genuinely care about it. But what if you don't care? Or what if you have a lot on your mind so you have trouble retaining information in the short term? The human mind chooses to dump any information that it does not find relevant and important to your overall life. Let's face it, a lot of the conversations you have are not that relevant or important. Therefore, it is hard to remember what you hear in conversation all of the time. Shocking or really important things might stick with you, but other details quickly fade away. You can certainly improve your ability to remember conversations by using some of the following tricks.

One trick to remembering what is said to you can be to think that you will narrate this whole conversation to someone else later on. While this may not be true, it tricks your mind into remembering what someone says to you better.

Another trick is to memorize important images that stand out to you in the conversation. If someone talks about what she expects from a lover, assign images to the things she says. You can assign flowers to romance, for instance. Then, you will be able to remember a series of images better than a long string of words.

The mind is often good at remembering emotions above all else. Therefore, you should try to remember the emotional textures of the conversation. What made the speaker very sad? What made you sad? Adding emotional charges to the conversation can help you remember its main themes better.

Now what about little details when you are getting to know someone? Things like birthdays are easy to forget. You are welcome to note these things down in a notebook or a notepad app on your phone while the details are still fresh in your mind. You can even whip out your phone and ask someone their birthday. This is one time when getting on your phone will make your conversation partner feel valued. He will love that you are trying so hard to remember a simple detail like his birthday.

Chapter 3: Reading People for Clues

First Impressions

First impressions are typically accurate. You should listen to your gut. Your subconscious mind is adept at picking out clues about people that your rational mind cannot possibly pick up on. Your gut will tell you the most accurate information about someone right off of the bat.

After you make a first impression, you may try to rationalize it. You may try to explain away negative feelings as poor judgment or jealousy. You may think that you read a person wrong. While these are vaguely possible, you will usually find out that your first impression was right in the end.

A good example is when you first meet a woman that you would like to be friends with. But your gut reaction to her is that she is not very nice. You decide to give her a chance since everyone else likes her and you get along after a while. After a while, however, you realize that all she does is say mean things about other people. Or she may betray you after years of friendship.

Your first impression is often all you have in business and situations like speed dating. So trust it. Your first impression is most likely correct, so act on it if you do not have time to get to know the person further.

Red Flags

There are some major red flags that automatically tell you that someone is toxic.

When you observe these traits or habits in someone, you know that someone is not good to be around. Run away when you spot these red flags. Do not try to somehow rationalize or justify these traits, as they are serious signs of underlying emotional issues or sociopathy.

Easy to Anger

A person who is easily ignited has anger problems. One day you will probably be the victim of his anger if you are not careful. Therefore, you should avoid people who are angered easily.

A history of violence is one sign that a person is easy to anger. Another sign is if he seems to demonstrate an angry posture. He will talk about fighting people or getting angry. He will immediately appear angry over the tiniest setbacks, such as his food being late at a restaurant.

Blaming Others

Right off the bat, you will notice if someone frequently blames others for what is wrong in his life. He will tell you all about how he is a victim. He will complain about how his ex-spouse cheated on him and brought about the divorce, he will blame getting fired recently on the fact that his former boss is just a huge jerk, and he will blame his recent car accident on the other stupid driver. Nothing will ever be his fault. He will claim that everyone else is responsible for his problems. And he will have plenty of problems to talk about. He will always be a victim.

Someone who plays the victim will probably one day accuse you of doing something wrong to him. He will never see how he is at fault. He will certainly never own up to his own bad actions or offer you any kind of apology.

Constant Complaining

A person who is very negative will just ooze that negativity through his speech. He will constantly complain about everything. It will appear as if the world is against him and nothing in life is good or worth doing. Just being around this person too long will make you feel depressed.

Sadly, many people are like this. They only see the bad in life. You can assume that a person like this will only bring you down. You will never be able to lighten someone like this up because he chooses to stay in a depressed mood.

Gossiping and Two-Facing

Some gossip is just human nature. Once you know someone well, a little bit of gossip now and then is normal. It is not a warning sign.

But when you first meet someone, the first thing you hear should not be a bunch of gossip about other people. A person who sits there talking about everyone else has a gossiping problem. He is obviously two-faced. Don't be fooled and think that you are the only one that he gossips to. Once you leave the room, he will start gossiping about you.

If someone gossips a lot, you want to watch what you say around him. You do not want to reveal too much, or it will become public information in two seconds. You also do not want to let his negativity sour you against other people. He will try to make you hate everyone else with the juicy, horrible details that he shares, but remember that gossip is rarely true. Even if it is, you do not have to be a part of this gossip's drama.

Women have the worst reputations as gossips. But men can be just as bad. Anyone who talks about other people a lot is a gossip. Be careful around such people.

Lacking Compassion

Have you ever met someone who laughs when other people fall? He seems to get some sick satisfaction from the suffering of others.

Even if he doesn't snicker at other people, he never demonstrates any remorse or compassion. When he speaks about other people, he uses very callous and cold language. When you point out someone's bad luck, for instance, he will snort and say that it is the person's own fault. This is the sign of a sociopath or psychopath. This person is very dangerous and certainly not the type of person that you want in your life.

The average person is capable of at least some compassion in conversation. He will feel bad when you mention that you are going through tough times or when someone falls, for instance. Someone who does not show any compassion and just ignores you or offers a callous remark when you say something that calls for compassion is not someone that you should associate with. If you do associate with this person, never expect him to show you compassion when you need it.

Things to Read

What He is Driven By

People are driven by various things. They will usually show what drives them by talking about it. For example, someone might say that he wants to go out to pick up chicks. Obviously sex drives him. Someone who frequently talks about money and making money is driven by financial security and wealth. Someone who talks about socializing a lot is an extrovert who is driven by having social interaction.

What drives a person can indicate what he wants from you. Read a person's language to gather clues about what he wants in life. His drive can indicate why he is seeking any sort of relationship with you, either professionally or personally. It also indicates what is important to him. If your goals align with his, then a relationship is a great idea. Otherwise, you may want to steer clear of this person.

What Feeds His Ego

Watch a person's ego to find out what feeds it. A lot of people are fed by accomplishments, such as making money or finishing a tough marathon. Some people are fed by flattery and being the object of desire. Some people are fed by sex and interactions with the opposite sex. What feeds someone's ego is apparent by what he talks about the most and what makes him smile.

Also, watch his responses to life situations. If a member of the opposite sex flirts with someone and his or her ego blossoms, you can assume that he or she has low self-esteem and requires lots of sexual attention to feel good. If he brags about his boat and other material possessions, you can tell that material success is what makes him feel complete.

If someone has a fragile ego that is fed by superficial things like material possessions and sexual attention, you can be sure that he has little confidence. The issues that come with insecurity are thus probably prevalent in this person. He will also do things to satisfy his own ego, and will chase after things and make stupid decisions just to keep his ego buoyed. Expect vices in someone like this.

But if someone's ego is fed by more solid things, such as his own accomplishments or the love of his family, then he is probably a secure and reliable person with healthy confidence and wholesome interests. You can trust someone like this to be a more solid companion in business or in your personal life.

What Stresses Him Out

Watch out for someone's stressors. Everyone has a source of stress. What a person complains about the most usually indicates what causes him the most emotional stress. If he complains about family, communication, commitment, and not always getting his way or not feeling loved may cause him stress. If he complains about work, his line of work and the tasks that he must do are probably not well-suited to his personality. If he seems to get quiet or upset in large crowds, you can assume that large crowds are not his forte.

Knowing what stresses someone out is very useful information. You can learn what to avoid doing around someone. You can become more sensitive to what someone does not like and also to situations that a person does not function well in. This is great information to know if you hire someone to work for you or if you begin dating someone.

What Pleases Him

People will go on and on about what makes them happy. You will most likely find out what makes someone happy relatively early in conversation. But you can also look for clues in what makes someone smile or what someone

fixates on with dilated pupils.

This is also useful to know. You learn

what you can do to please someone. This can

make you a better lover, friend, or even employer

and co-worker.

How Does He Behave Under Stress

How someone handles stress says a lot

about how he will treat you when things get

hard. Life can throw a lot of challenges your way,

so you usually want people around who can

handle stress well. If a stressful situation arises

and someone literally falls apart or gets fiercely

angry, just know that he is probably not a

reliable friend during times of stress. He is also

not a good prospect in a stressful line of

business. On the other hand, if he is able to remain calm and collected under stress, he is someone that you can rely on in the future.

Chapter 4: What Isn't Said Aloud: Reading Facial Expressions and Body Language

Leaning

People lean forward to things that they like or feel attracted to you. It is a good sign when someone leans toward you. If someone is really listening to you or really likes you, he will lean toward you or position his torso to face you.

However, if someone leans his torso away from you, that indicates that he is going through some type of stress. Either he does not like what you are saying, or he is having some sort of negative reaction to you as a person. This reaction is also not always directed toward you. You may also notice someone pulling away from you and leaning away from you if he receives bad

63

news in a text message or phone call or sees something that distresses him.

Hands

Really watch someone's hands. What he does with his hands indicate a lot about what he is feeling. His hand movements are an even better indicator of deception than his eye contact.

Fidgeting or constant hand movements indicate intense nervousness. If someone tries to make smoothing gestures with his hands, he is probably lying. If he is balling his hands into fists, that indicates aggression.

Fidgeting and Pacifying Gestures

Fidgeting is a sign of nervousness and emotional distress. Picking at one's nails, rubbing one's thighs or forehead, and scooting around in one's seat are some of the forms of fidgeting that indicate that someone is experiencing some sort of emotional duress. This emotional duress may be related to the conversation. It may be because he is lying to you and feels guilty and nervous about getting caught. It may even be because he is going through something bad in his life and it is manifesting even though he is trying to focus on talking to you.

Especially watch for pacifying gestures. This is any kind of rubbing or smoothing motion that a person performs on his own body. When someone rubs himself in any way, he is trying to soothe himself. Consider what he may be trying to soothe himself about. If you are talking about his job and he starts rubbing his forehead while telling you that everything at work is stellar, you can assume that there are problems in his work life. If he repeatedly rubs his thighs while bragging about what a great guy he is, you can safely assume that he is thinking of all the ways that he has been a bad guy and he is trying to soothe his guilt. When you bring up a subject such as divorce, you can tell that someone is distressed by the topic by his sudden influx of pacifying gestures. A person who is constantly trying to pacify himself during a normal conversation is probably socially anxious.

If someone touches the crook of his neck, this is a gesture of discomfort and even fear. The throat is vulnerable, so when a person grabs at it or touches the crook of it, this is a self-defensive gesture. This gesture can show that a person feels threatened by you or someone else that he is talking to. Also, this gesture is most common in women rather than men. Watch for women who perform this fidgety gesture around their husbands or boyfriends as a clue about abuse.

Facial Expressions

Facial expressions essentially leak someone's internal emotions. This leakage is very hard for people to control. Most people can't control it and their initial reactions to things will flash across their faces before they regain control and put on their normal social mask of a smile or serious frown.

If you bring up a subject and you notice that someone suddenly clenches his jaw or furrows his brow, you can assume that the subject upsets him in some way. A person who attempts to act serene or happy yet keeps clenching his jaw is probably either an aggressive person at heart or has something upsetting on his mind that he is not telling you about. Tense facial expressions in someone's baseline often indicate that someone is naturally tense and aggressive, insecure, or often depressed.

If you notice a brief smile, you can tell that something brings someone great pleasure. Watch for brief flashes of mirth when you are talking about upsetting or serious subjects. This can indicate that a person gets sadistic pleasure from the upsetting subject matter. This is a troubling sign of sociopathy or psychopathy. Alternatively, if someone can't hide his mirth at a serious matter, you can assume that he doesn't take things seriously and lacks proper respect.

Facial expressions tend to leave their marks on people's faces. Most people adopt a general mood based on their outlook on life. This general mood is reflected in a general facial expression. As people wear certain expressions over time, these expressions carve permanent wrinkles or grooves into their facial tissue. People who are often depressed will have frown lines in their brow and on either side of their mouths. People who are generally jovial will have laugh lines and dimples from smiling. People who are often angry will have tense lines around their eyes and a hard gaze. Lines along the top of the nose can indicate someone who is frequently wrinkling up his nose in disgust and hence is a very critical and judgmental person.

Silence

If someone takes a long pause, clears their throat, or falls silent, then they are trying to think of what to say. They may be stalling for time as they manufacture the best response. They may just be waiting for you to offer guidelines about where the conversation should go.

Silence is not always bad. You should listen to your gut about it. If there is an uneasy vibe with the silence, then you can safely assume that the silence is not natural and easy. If there is a comfortable vibe, don't doubt that and make yourself nervous. You can enjoy silence with someone if it feels right to you.

Eye Contact

Eyes are considered windows into the soul because of the wealth of information that they provide about a person's emotional state and feelings toward you. Eye contact helps maintain emotional connection between people. Changes in eye contact can break the connection or show problems within it.

When someone closes his eyes, this is a sign that he is thinking really hard about his response and is stalling for time. This does not necessarily mean that he is thinking of a lie. But it can mean that this subject is difficult for him to talk about, either emotionally or mentally, and he needs time to think of the perfect words.

A lack of eye contact can indicate that someone is not comfortable in what he is telling you. This is not necessarily a sign of deceit. It could just be a sign of nervousness or shyness. It can also be a sign that someone feels ashamed of something. A lack of eye contact is often cited as an accurate way to spot deception, but in fact good liars are perfectly able to maintain normal eye contact while lying. Eye contact is not the best gauge of deception.

Piercing eye contact can make you uncomfortable, and for good reason. Someone who looks into your eyes too piercingly is likely searching you for information. He may be trying to force a connection on false grounds. Too much eye contact is a better indicator of deception than lack of eye contact, as a matter of fact.

Pupils

Another clue that eye contact can offer is pupil dilation. If someone's pupils dilate around you, that is a sign that he likes you or likes what you are saying. During a business meeting, you may notice that your client's pupils dilate when he hears that he is about to make bank on a new product if he chooses to invest. When you are trying to sell something, pupil dilation indicates that someone is interested. Watch for pupil dilation in your dates, too, to tell if they really like you.

Pupil constriction means the opposite. When someone's pupils constrict, he isn't happy with what he sees. He is displeased and pulling away emotionally. He may be upset and bothered or seriously offended. Watch for pupil constriction in people when you bring up unpleasant subject matter or when a gruesomely violent scene occurs during a movie.

Breath

Someone's breathing rates indicates his heart rate. His heart rate indicates his emotional state. Someone who is calm will have normal, level breathing, while someone who is upset will have more rapid breathing.

Do not read too much into breath, however. Some people have health issues that affect their breathing rates. Exercise, high wind, allergies, and other factors can all make someone breathe heavily around you. However, you cannot ignore things like heavy exhales or sharp inhales. These indicate someone's immediate emotional response to something.

A sharp inhale often shows that someone is shocked or surprised. A long, heavy exhale means that someone feels defeated and is under intense emotional distress. Often a liar will make this exhale when he has been caught in a lie.

Walking

How a person walks suggests a lot about his confidence and what he is feeling. A confident person walks with big, firm gestures and keeps his spine straight and his head held up straight. You want to deal with confident people, as they know how to take care of themselves.

Less confident people will shrink into themselves. Their shoulders will be hunched, their heads will be held down, and their spines will be slouched. They will probably shuffle along, trying to avoid attracting too much attention.

A person who is sad may also walk like this. A happy person will bounce along, showing his joy in big movements. An angry person will usually be tense, with his fists balled up and his shoulders forced up.

Chapter 5: Guessing Peoples' Hidden Intentions

Deceit

Wouldn't it be nice if you could tell when people are lying to you? Your lie detector will become much stronger if you watch for these signs in people. Once you are able to determine when people are lying, you possess a great deal of power. You can really encourage honesty and you can offer consequences to the liars in your life.

Most people do lie. The worst liars in your life are probably people that you actually know quite well. Your significant other is shown in studies to be the most likely to lie to you. From little white lies to keep the relationship healthy to big lies about where he or she was last night, you can expect your lover to lie. But family members and friends and business partners are all equally capable of lying as well. Many people use deception as a means for survival; lying is shown to start as early as infancy. You don't have to tolerate lying, however. Demand that people respect your intelligence and treat you with integrity and honesty.

Difference from the Baseline

Marked differences in someone's behavior from his usual baseline is a good indicator that deception is going on. His gestures, body language, eye contact, and tone will differ from the usual. You will wonder why he is acting so strangely. The likely answer is that he is being less than truthful with you.

Quavering Voice

Someone who is nervous and suffering from a lot of emotional tension will have a quavering voice. It is difficult for most people to tell bold, direct lies. So when they do, they have a lot of trouble talking to you directly. They won't want to speak in a normal, confident tone because they lack confidence in what they are saying.

Sweating

Lying takes a lot of effort. The thought of getting caught is quite scary. Therefore, a liar is often under intense emotional stress while lying. He will start sweating. You will notice beads of sweat forming on his face, particularly along his brow and temples. If he frequently wipes at this sweat to hide it from you, that is an even greater affirmation that he is lying.

Grooming and Cleaning Gestures

A liar can feel dirty from his lies if he has a conscience. Therefore, he will try to placate his sense of dirtiness by performing grooming gestures. He may smooth out his tie or the wrinkles in his pants. He may pick at his nails, inspecting them for cleanliness. He may even groom his hair or facial hair. The key to watch for is when he does these things while talking to you. His grooming habits will interest him much more than looking right at you.

In addition, neatening or organizing things while talking to you also indicates deception. A liar will straighten out stacks of paper on the desk in front of him or will preoccupy himself with cleaning things while avoiding looking at you. A lie can make someone feel disorganized, as someone attempts to straighten out his story. Therefore, his efforts to create a neat and tight story will manifest in him organizing things around him.

Mismatched Cues

His gestures and body language will not match his words. He may be saying that he is happy, but the unhappy droop in his shoulders will alert you otherwise. He may be saying that he is not lying to you, but meanwhile he is hiding his hands from you.

Usually people are consistent between their nonverbal and verbal communication.

Inconsistencies are cause for alarm. When an inconsistency exists, someone is experiencing a mismatch between what he says and what he feels. This is a good sign that he is not telling the truth. You can spot even tiny white lies this way.

Mismatched Verb Tenses

Most people tell their stories in a specific order: back story, main content, and aftermath. Most people will use the past tense, since the story occurred in the past. If at any point during the story someone switches to a different tense, namely the present tense, then you have a good indication that something is not entirely truthful in the story that he is telling.

A person will switch to the present tense because his mind is busy manufacturing details in the present as he tells the story. Therefore, the present tense often indicates that a story is not truthful. Rather, it is made up on the spot.

Descriptive Vagueness

Remember how I said liars have a tough time being direct? A liar will be very vague in his language because he has trouble being direct due to his lack of honesty. Therefore, watch for intentionally vague language and word choice.

For instance, if you are accusing an employee of not locking the doors to your store last night, she may lie and say, "But I swear that the door got locked." Notice how vague that statement is. She doesn't directly say that she herself locked the door. She uses the passive term "got locked."

A liar will try to remove himself from blame or from a situation that he does not want to be implicated in. He will do this with more passive language. A person who is being honest will usually use more direct and non-passive language.

Lessening the Impact

A liar will try to lessen the impact of what he is being accused of by choosing words that carry softer connotations. Someone who is lying may choose a word like "taken" over "stolen," or "stepped out" instead of "cheated." He will pick words that make what he did seem less offensive. This is his way of trying to lessen the impact of what he did and trying to convince you that what you are upset about is not that big of a deal. He is essentially trying to take the heat off of himself. But don't fall for this.

Defensiveness

A liar will get defensive if you confront him. Instead of just saying that he is being honest, he will try to manipulate you into feeling bad for doubting his honesty. He will say things like, "Why wouldn't you believe me?" or "Would I lie to you?" He may also act angry and ask why you have the nerve to question his integrity.

Some key terms to watch out for include:

"Why would I lie?"

"Would I ever lie to you?"

"You know me. I'm not a liar. And I hate the accusation."

"Have I ever lied to you?"

"Why wouldn't you believe me?"

"You can believe me or not. It's your choice."

"I swear to God/I swear on my mother's grave."

"You won't believe me, I know, but I wouldn't lie about this."

An honest person may get defensive too. But this is because he is desperate to get you to believe him. He will probably say things more like, "I am being honest," or "I am an honest person. Please believe me."

Sharp Exhale

A sharp exhale can indicate when someone has been caught. If you confront someone about something and he sharply exhales, you can assume that he is probably guilty. An exhale is an automatic reaction that many people have to getting caught in some sort of lie or other action. It is a sign of emotional distress, often guilt.

Clusters of Actions

Often, a single action does not offer very much information about someone. But clusters of actions can really tell you if someone is lying. A liar will usually have more than just one tell. Watch for several aberrations in behavior to clue you in on his honesty.

Manipulation

Have you ever met a seemingly really nice person, then find out that he or she is just using you? After a while, you start to notice that you are being manipulated. You get that yucky feeling that you don't matter to the person. Well, you can avoid that yucky feeling altogether by recognizing when someone is manipulating you.

Manipulators are typically emotionally stuck in childhood. They have never developed the proper adult skills of communication. Because of how they were raised, they found that playing games were more effective at getting them what they wanted than just asking. But they never outgrew this and adjusted to normal adulthood. Now, they feel that they must play games.

On the other hand, some manipulators are sociopaths. They have literally no empathy or compassion for others. They view other people as tools that they can use to their own ends.

No matter why someone is manipulative, you do not deserve that kind of treatment. You are not a pawn for someone to use. You should learn to identify this behavior to avoid a lot of problems and hurt in the future. Remember that you can never change a manipulator. Besides, it is not your job to heal or change a manipulator.

Flattery

A manipulator will be great at making you feel like you need him in your life. He gets an emotional hook into you by first making you feel like you depend on him for your happiness. He will flatter you and charm you until you just can't get enough.

However, this flattery is all fake. Somewhere in your gut you will probably feel that is fake. Whether you feel that eerie sense that something is not right or not, just be very wary of someone who is too nice.

Lots of Small Favors

Watch out for someone who is extremely generous right after meeting you. Usually a stranger is not so nice. Therefore, a lot of small favors is a bad sign. It means that someone is trying to put you in his debt. He is doing you a lot of favors to get you to feel like you must do things for him in return. He is essentially collecting favors to call on for later.

Threats

The other trick that a manipulator uses is getting you to feel too scared to do anything without him in your life. Whether he is a romantic partner or a business partner, he will use threats to make you feel like only he would want to be around you. He will make it seem like you are a horrible person and only he is able to put up with you. He will do this so that you feel as if you cannot do anything without him. You feel that he is the only one who will tolerate you, so that you never leave the situation with him.

A manipulative person will start doing this relatively quickly after meeting you. He knows that in reality he is a terrible person with little to offer you. Therefore, he will want to ensure that you never leave him and move on to someone better for love, business, friendship, or anything else.

Drama

A manipulator will try to create a lot of drama in your life. By creating drama, his aim is to get you to relent to what he wants just to end the drama. He tries to make your life miserable until you give in.

He may also try to create drama in order to drive away your loved ones and friends. That way, he can isolate you. When you are isolated, you are vulnerable. You have no one to protect you or tell you that you are being treated wrongly. A manipulator likes to have you in this spot so that he can exploit you.

Guilt

One of the most powerful human emotions is guilt. Guilt will make you do things just to escape the feeling. Manipulators understand this fact. As a result, they love to use guilt to make you feel bad so that you do what they want. They are fantastic at making you feel guilty just for being alive.

If someone frequently makes you feel guilty or ashamed, then you are being manipulated. No one who cares about you will make you feel this way. A stranger certainly has no right to make you feel this way. Watch for people that frequently bring up your mistakes, tell you that you are a bad person, or tell you that you are somehow inadequate. Watch for people who act put upon when you ask them to do things, so that you feel guilty just for asking.

These are all signs of manipulation and you should run far away when you encounter them, especially in people that you just meet.

Behaving Unbearably

Another form of manipulation is when a person throws a childish fit rather than acting like an adult. He will sulk, pout, yell, or otherwise act like a jerk until you do what he wants. He gets his way by making you miserable. You finally do what he wants just to get him to stop.

An example of this is when you want to go to a certain restaurant to meet someone. He doesn't really want to go there. But instead of telling you that, he comes along to the restaurant and then pouts the entire time. He makes you so miserable that you finally just want to leave the restaurant.

He Won't Tell You Things to Your Face

If a manipulator is unhappy about something, he will not have the strength to tell you to your face. Instead, he will tell everyone else in the world but you. He will make sure that it gets back to you through other people how unhappy he is. In this way, he tells you how unhappy he is without having to tell you himself. He avoids confrontation in a very chicken way.

For example, someone might tell you that he is happy to work for you late. But then he complains to the entire office about how you shoved off your workload on him. You find out how unhappy he is to work for you from everyone in the office. He could have just told you no to your face.

Lying

A manipulator is usually also a liar. If you frequently catch someone lying to you, you should watch out. You do not need liars in your life. But usually a liar brings loads of other problems along with him.

Refusing to Take Blame

If someone does something bad to you, you will naturally want to confront him. But if he immediately twists what he did to you to seem like your fault, then he is manipulative. He will be adept at making you feel as if everything is your fault. He will have an amazing way of always escaping blame. Also, he will never, ever admit to wrongdoing and he will never say that he is sorry for anything.

Chapter 6: Looking at Clues in Someone's Life

When it comes to reading people, sometimes you cannot learn a lot about a person based just on how he acts on a first meeting. Behavior can be extremely deceptive, especially during a first meeting when someone is putting on the charm for you. But watching someone's behavior over time and observing someone's past for clues about their general behavior can give you a lot of clues about a person's real personality.

Past Behavior

You should get to know a person the best that you can. That way, you can observe patterns in his general behavior. You can also hear more and more stories about his past, as well. Generally, someone will open up to you and tell you about his past. From his past behavior, you can gather a lot of clues about who he is.

A long string of bad relationships or several divorces are one warning sign that he is unable to be a sensitive and communicative lover. It is likely that he is unable to learn from his mistakes, as well. If he has a lot of enemies, that suggests that he is a hard person to get along with and he may be a traitorous personality. A history of spending money frivolously, large amounts of debt, poor financial decisions, and gambling indicate poor planning and an inability to handle his life. Someone who frequently gets into trouble with the law by fighting or other behavior has poor impulse and poor emotional control. If he frequently bails on plans and doesn't demonstrate any follow-through, then he is probably not someone to trust with any serious commitment in business or even romance and family. One thing to really watch out for is someone who has kids with many different people. This shows a huge lack of responsibility and an inability to commit.

It is true that people can change. Just because someone screwed up when he was younger does not mean that you should judge him for the rest of his life. However, repeated behavior indicates that he never learned from his mistakes. This is very troubling. Even if he says that he has learned his lessons, his repetition of the same mistakes is living proof that he has not. Watch for repeated mistakes or very recent mistakes that show that he has not really changed.

Earlier I mentioned that you should never judge someone based off of behavior only. While this holds true, repeated behavior is something that you can safely judge. A person who does the same things over and over is likely rooted in such behavior. Watch how someone frequently acts around you. Watch for patterns in behavior. Patterns should never be ignored.

Reputation

What other people say is not always reliable. You can't believe everything that you hear on the rumor mill. Sometimes, people will have a vendetta against someone and will spread vicious rumors. Sometimes, just one person is able to spread enough false information about another person to create his bad reputation.

But usually, a large number of people don't conspire against one person. If you hear several people say the same thing about someone, you might want to listen. It is probably true. A person gains a reputation over time by doing the same thing to many people. A reputation is a good thing to pay attention to. The odds are that if someone is repeatedly bad to other people, he will be bad to you.

Meanwhile, a good reputation is an encouraging sign. Someone who gains a reputation as being honest or nice is usually really that way. However, don't rely on reputation alone. Someone may be good at pulling the wool over everyone's eyes. You might be able to read bad things in him that no one else can. Trust your gut in this scenario. Just because everyone else likes someone does not mean that you should, too. Sometimes the most upstanding citizens are hiding very dark secrets and underneath their honest reputations they have dirty souls.

Conclusion

Now you know how to read people like a book. Your life will become so much easier now that you have finished this book and learned the critical life skill of reading other people.

You can become a better person by knowing how to read people. Reading people allows you to develop empathy. You can tell what others are feeling and respond accordingly. Your sensitivity will make you a more responsive and caring lover, parent, friend, and family member.

You can also protect yourself better from the harm of people with bad intentions. When you are able to read people, you are consequently able to spot people that will not benefit you. Before you get too far into a relationship of any nature with someone harmful, you can see what the person is about and prevent further harm from happening.

When it comes to choosing a good friend or lover, you are now better able to pick people that are good for your life. You can spot those that actually care for you and have the capability of treating you well. You can pick lovers and friends that have good track records.

All of these benefits are now yours.

Thanks for reading.

Other great books by Madison Taylor on Kindle, paperback and audio

Rejection Proof Therapy 101: How To Overcome, Deal With And Heal Yourself From Rejection

Cognitive Behavioral Therapy For Beginners: How To Use CBT To Overcome Anxieties,

Phobias, Addictions, Depression, Negative Thoughts, And Other Problematic Disorders

Forbidden Psychology 101: The Cool Stuff They Didn't Teach You About In School

Escaping the Introvert World: The Introvert's Guide To Overcoming Shyness, Social Anxiety, And Fear To Thrive In An Extrovert World

NLP For Beginners: Learn the Secrets of Self Mastery, Developing Magnetic Influence and Reaching Your Goals Using Neuro-Linguistic Programming

Depression Proof Yourself: How To Avoid And Overcome Being Depressed

Love Thyself: The First Commandment to Raising your Self Esteem, Boosting your Self-Confidence, and Increasing your Happiness

The Art of Decision Making: How to Make Better Choices in Love, Life, and Work

The Dark Science of Psychological Warfare: How To Always Keep The Upper Hand On Anyone Psychologically

Staying Focused: How to Effectively Eliminate the Weapons of Mass Distraction

Turbo Charged NLP: A New and Improved Way of Taking Self Mastery, Influence, and Neuro-linguistic Programming to the Next Level

The Art of Deception: How To Master And Use Subterfuge On Anyone

How to Deal with Difficult People

Conquering the Fear of Failure: How to Overcome Your Fears and Achieve Anything You Set Your Mind To